TheMarketingGuru.ca Presents...

Writing Marketing, Strategic, and Business Plans

by
Don Curtis

Contents

WRITING YOUR MARKETING PLAN

100 question format for ease of use.

You won't find this kind of practical know-how in a textbook!

Let's start with a simple truth.

Write the following sentence and put your product name in the blank. Remind yourself of this fact daily.

The world is not about _____, it is about people.

For some reason, many companies fear the word *marketing*, equating it with spending vast amounts of money on advertising, PR, etc. But marketing isn't about advertising, PR, websites, emails, etc. -- Those are merely the tools of marketing.

Marketing is 100% about the market...your market and understanding it fully.

It is the planning and execution of all the production, pricing, promotion and distribution of goods and services to create purchase by your customers.

It is matching every part of your business with your customers' needs and wants and with their motivation to purchase.

It is not just a matter of selling; it addresses what is to be sold, how it is to be sold, when, where and at what price.

If the marketing plan is working, all facets of the business will be harnessed and focused towards the achievement of customer satisfaction.

It is the function of the plan to identify the customer, establish their needs and, by coordinating the efforts of all sections of the business, bring about sales.

Marketing, simply put, is everything about your product from **conception** to **consumption** and all the steps in between. It is selling the **right product** to the **right people** at the **right time** and at the **right price**. In other words, the marketing plan helps you get it **RIGHT**.

Rule one:
Failing to plan is planning to fail.

A wise sage once said, "There is nothing so uncommon as common sense."

I repeat that here because marketing is, for the most part, just good common sense. And if you keep that in mind, the job is a lot simpler.

Your plan will determine what your business should become and how to achieve that goal. And it will put everyone in the organization on the same page. There are two main components of the plan.

1.   How you will address the market; and,
2.   How you will implement and support the operation.

And remember that it is futile to have a plan that you have neither the resources nor the expertise to execute. (This is a very common problem!)

Purposes of a Marketing Plan

One of the key purposes of the plan is to ensure consistency of all your sales/promotion endeavours.

In addition to defining marketing strategy, you must have a well defined methodology for the day to day implementation of the plan.

Other benefits are:

- A rallying point for staff, to make them feel part of the team and to give the team direction.
- Chart to success -- a step-by-step guide to success.
- Company operational discussions -- a to-do list on a grand scale.
- Captured thinking -- the plan is there to remind everyone of the goal.
- Top level reflection -- writing the plan is your chance and that of your senior executives to look at the big picture. It forces you to look internally and to fully understand the results of past decisions. It forces the marketing personnel to look externally at the market in which they operate.

- It provides a concrete set of goals that can be reviewed over time.

A good marketing plan sets clear, precise and measurable targets.

It includes deadlines.

It provides a budget for each marketing activity.

It specifies who is responsible for implementation and follow-up of every activity.

****

And remember that a plan will not execute itself:

It needs to be a living document.
It needs a champion.
It needs to be reviewed -- often.
(Never forget the above six points!)

Getting Started

Let's start with some devilishly simple questions.
The questions are simple...the answers are not.

1. Is there a customer demand for your product?

    _____

2. How deep is that demand?

    _____

    _____

3. Can you satisfy the demand from both psychological and production standpoints?

    _____

4. Who and what influences the demand?

    _____

    _____

5. What and who is already out there? Who is the competition and what do they offer?

_____

_____

_____

6. How are they positioned? (List each.)

_____

_____

_____

_____

7. What is the customers' view of their product?

_____

_____

_____

_____

8. What "space" does your product occupy in the customer mind? (Now)

_____

_____

9. What "space" can you occupy? (e.g., better product, better price, new technology, better delivery, etc.)

_____

_____

10. Who wants your product?

_____

_____

11. How big is the potential market?

_____

12. What do you know and don't know about the market?

_____

_____

_____

_____

13. How readily can you get the information and how will you get it?

_____

_____

14. Will you go directly to prospects and ask them (market research) or is the data available from trade groups, existing surveys, etc.?

_____

_____

_____

15. Can you prepare a buyer profile? Who are they, where are they, what do they want, what need are you satisfying, how does your product help their business/life, etc.?

_____

_____

_____

_____

_____

Bottom line: the better you know the customer, the more effective and efficient (read less expensive) your marketing will be.

16. How long is the sales cycle and how will this affect your cash flow?

_____

_____

17. What are your sales channels?

_____

_____

_____

18. What is your brand?

_____

19. What does it stand for?

_____

20. What is its current image?

_____

_____

_____

21. What do you want it to be?

_____

_____

22. How will you position your brand in the marketplace and in customers' minds?

_____

_____

_____

23. Can you answer the question: "What do you do and why should I care?" in 20 seconds or less?

_____

_____

_____

_____

24. How well can you target your prospects?

_____

_____

25. What media will you use?

_____

_____

_____

26. How much, how often?

_____

_____

27. How will you ensure consistency of message, look, brand, etc., across all media?

_____

_____

_____

28. How are you going to measure success?

_____

_____

29. Have you set realistic and attainable goals?

_____

_____

See, I told you that the questions were simple, but the answers hard!

So, now that you've thought about all that and answered the questions (you have, haven't you?), let's get started on your marketing plan...

The Marketing Plan will consist of the following sections:

A. Executive Summary
B. Business Overview
C. Mission Statement
D. Corporate Objective
E. Corporate Strategy
F. Market Audit -- Target Market
G. SWOT Analysis -- Strengths, Weaknesses, Opportunities, Threats
H. Assumptions
I. Marketing Objectives and Strategies
J. Budget/Financial Summary
K. Communications Plan
L. Media Plan
M. Distribution Plan
N. Customer Analysis
O. Product Features/Benefits
P. Evaluation

Executive Summary

30. What are your main goals? Highlight the main goals and recommendations, along with how success will be measured.

_____

_____

_____

_____

_____

_____

31. Clearly define what you do. What is my company about, and why are you in business? Sounds easy, doesn't it. But it isn't.

_____

_____

_____

_____

_____

_____

32. All your marketing efforts are ultimately directed at answering one key customer question: "What's in it for me?" Try and answer their question.

_____

_____

_____

_____

_____

Business Overview

33. Relevant background on the market, product, pricing, and distribution situations.

_____

_____

_____

_____

_____

_____

_____

34. If an existing business, recap last twelve months: customer base, environmental factors, size and growth of the market, sales, gross margins, net profits, description of major competitors and their actions and rank. Psychological, technological, geographic, and economic changes during the year.

_____

_____

_____

_____

_____

_____

_____

_____

_____

_____

Mission Statement

35. A clear, concise statement of how you want your product/service to be represented and perceived by your customers. The positioning strategy focuses on the target market segments the business seeks to serve, and the differentiating advantage with which it will compete with rivals in the segment.

_____

_____

_____

_____

_____

_____

_____

Corporate Objective

36. What you intend to do. If you are one of the strongest competitors, then your objective is to invest the best resources. If you are a new or weaker competitor, your objective might be to concentrate on strengthening the company using the product to achieve the objective of becoming a stronger player, etc.

_____

_____

_____

_____

_____

Corporate Strategy

37. Usually falls into one of three categories:

    i)   Cost leader
    ii) Differentiation -- product is unique across the industry -- technology, image, special features, superior service, better distribution, etc.
    iii) Focus -- on a particular segment of the market.

_____

_____

_____

_____

Market Audit

The more you know about your customers, the more efficient and effective your plan!

38. Who are your customers?

_____

_____

39. How can you get their attention?

_____

_____

40. Where do they get their information?

_____

_____

41. What motivates them to buy?

_____

_____

_____

42. What is important to them?

_____

_____

_____

_____

_____

Conduct focus groups, phone surveys, etc.
Knowledge is king, and money spent up front on
understanding your target will save you thousands
in marketing costs and errors later!

SWOT Analysis

43. In answering the SWOT analysis, it is
     mandatory to be brutally honest with
     yourself. Pretending that you don't have
     weaknesses or overplaying your strengths is
     a bad idea. Give yourself a shake, and dig
     in...

Strengths

_____

_____

_____

_____

Weaknesses

_____

_____

_____

_____

Opportunities

_____

_____

_____

_____

Threats (to Success)

_____

_____

_____

_____

44. Are you selling to existing customers or new ones?

_____

45. How aware are they of your product and its benefits?

_____

46. What is the growth rate of the market segments?

_____

47. How much time does it take for the customer to make a decision?

_____

48. Are they willing to pay a higher price for a better product?

_____

49. How many people are involved in the purchase decision and who are they?

_____

_____

50. What risks are involved in their purchase?

_____

_____

51. Are they prepared to pay for value? And, of
     course, that value will depend on their
     knowledge of your product, the competition,
     quality, durability, reliability, and the
     significance of the benefits.

_____

_____

_____

_____

52. The 4 Ps:

Product: quality, features, name, packaging,
services, guarantees

_____

_____

_____

_____

Price: list, discounts, allowances, credit

_____

_____

_____

_____

Promotion: advertising, personal selling, sales promos, public relations, webpage, trade shows...What mix will you see?

_____

_____

_____

_____

Place: distributors, retailers, locations, inventory, transport, warehousing...How/where does the customer get your product?

_____

_____

_____

_____

Assumptions

About the market, the competition, the product, etc.

53.   Are the features of your product proprietary?

_____

54.   What benefits do the customers get by using it?

_____

_____

55.   How are you differentiated from competition? Is it readily apparent?

_____

_____

_____

56.   How will you assure quality control?

_____

_____

57. How quickly can your benefit be copied? How long until the benefit is obsolete? What is your plan to continually stay ahead? What is the product's potential for improvement?

_____

_____

_____

_____

_____

58. How complex is your offering: options, installation, tech support?

_____

_____

59. Do you have the management team to do the job and stay the course?

_____

_____

60. Do you have the capacity to make critical decisions without undue influence from distributors, retailers, etc.?

_____

_____

61. Is the product free from legal hassles?

_____

62. How good is your customer service?

_____

_____

_____

Marketing Objectives and Strategies

63. Objectives -- What do you intend to do?
    What do you want to achieve?

_____

_____

_____

_____

_____

_____

_____

64. Strategies -- How do you intend to do it? List tasks to be accomplished to implement the plan and assign an actual person to be responsible. Give each a time frame.

        Task   Responsibility   Timeframe

i) _____

ii) _____

iii) _____

iv) _____

v) _____

Budget/Financial Summary

No marketing plan is complete without a quantitative projection of profitability for the product, and you will have to project a sales forecast.

65. How much will it cost to achieve the objectives and execute the strategies?

_____

_____

66. Pro forma -- cost of production and sale.

(Attach.)

67. Pricing strategy -- market penetration price -- comparable price -- exclusive price.

(Attach.)

68. Do your competitors have the resources to retaliate?

_____

69. Do you have the strength to limit suppliers' bargaining powers?

_____

_____

70. Can you sustain market position?

_____

71. Have you double-checked all numbers in the plan?

_____

Communications Plan

Why advertise? The product positioning, competitive features and customer benefits are the basics of your advertising proposition. It makes the name of your company and product known to potential customers, creates goodwill, builds a positive image, educates and informs, offers specific attributes, attracts customers, gives them a reason to purchase.

No plan is complete unless it addresses the future!

Consistency across all materials will maximize impact and save dollars.

72. Advertising -- where, what and how much?

_____

_____

_____

_____

73. Will it help achieve long-term goals?

_____

74. Will it build up long-term strengths?

_____

75. What effect will I have on other products?

_____

_____

76. Public Relations – getting your story out. How/where/who is responsible?

_____

_____

77. Promotion:

_____

78. Website/Social Media:

_____

79. Packaging:

_____

80. Point of Sale:

_____

81. Brochures, etc.:

_____

Selling the benefits...Customers won't buy a bad product more than once. They will not buy a product if they don't understand how it benefits them. And they will not buy a product if they are confused by it or its message, image, or positioning. If your product has benefits, then make sure they are front and centre in your communications and clearly explained.

Media Plan

82. Where are your prospects?

_____

_____

_____

83. Which media will reach them efficiently, what time of year, frequency of message, etc.? (Fish where the fish are!)

_____

_____

_____

_____

_____

Distribution Plan

84. Premise sales, direct sales, wholesale
     channel, self-service channel, full service
     channel.

_____

_____

_____

_____

Customer Analysis

85. How well do you know your customers?

_____

_____

86. What type of product features appeal to your
     key customers?

_____

_____

87. How are choices made between
     competitors?

_____

_____

88. How much do they have to spend on your product?

_____

_____

89. How do they reach decisions to purchase?

_____

_____

90. Are they pre-sold?

_____

91. Which media do they watch/read/listen to?

_____

_____

92. Where are they?

_____

_____

93. What are their information needs?

_____

_____

94. What do they need versus what do you
currently offer?

_____

_____

95. Are there groups who are not buying your
product? Why?

_____

_____

_____

Product Features/Benefits

It is important to make a clear distinction between
the features of competing products.

96. List features.

_____

_____

_____

97. Do the features of your product lead to a
unique positioning?

_____

_____

Evaluation

98. What are the criteria for success?

_____

_____

99. How will you measure success?

_____

_____

_____

100. Have all your senior executives/department heads signed off on the plan?

_____

The Marketing Plan is part of the Business Plan and links with it. Your business plan spells out what your business is about, what you do and don't do, what your ultimate goals are.   It encompasses more than marketing.   It can include discussions of location, staffing, financing, strategic alliances, etc.   It includes a vision that spells out the purpose of the company.

Good luck. And get writing!

DEVELOPING YOUR STRATEGIC PLAN

Vision, Mission, Content, SWOT,
Implementation, Getting Started, 3 Phases.

Plus 16 key questions to get you there.

Let's start with a few definitions.

What is a strategic plan?

1. It is a document that clearly sets out where your organization is going, how it is going to get there, why it exists and what it is trying to accomplish.

2. It is a set of decisions about what to do, why to do it and how to do it. Typically, it will encompass your entire organization.

Queen to Alice: "Now, see, it takes all the running you can do to keep in the same place; if you want to get somewhere, you have to run at least twice as fast as that." -- Lewis Carroll, Alice's Adventures in Wonderland

A Strategic Plan is NOT a Business Plan

It is a concise, systematic way to develop a course of action and direction for your company. A Business Plan is much more comprehensive – it includes the strategic plan, marketing plan, financial plan and operational plan.

Why do you need a strategic plan?

- It is a framework for decisions.
- It is a basis for more detailed planning.
- It explains your business to others.
- It is a benchmark for performance.
- It stimulates change.
- It is a building block for future plans.

Mock Turtle to Alice: "I've never heard it before, but it sounds uncommon nonsense."

Mission Statement

- A mission statement communicates the essence of your business.
- It is a brief written statement of the purpose of your organization.
- It is a broad description of who and what you are, the nature and purpose of your business...it's a raison d'etre.
- Who you are.

- What you do -- The business you engage in. What are your products/ services?
- What industry are you in?
- What markets do you serve?
- What is its major driving force?
- Why you are doing it?
- The purpose of your company.
- What you seek to accomplish.
- What activities it will perform and how?
- What you will really be doing.
- What makes it special.
- A statement of values.
- What the ultimate result of your work will be.
- Maximum 150 words -- and every verb and noun must count!

Eaglet to Alice: "Speak English, I don't know the meaning of half of those big words, and I don't believe you do, either."

What is a vision statement?

A vision statement is the guiding image of success, a blueprint for the organization's work.

What is our preferred future?

What will the business look like in the future? It:

- incorporates your beliefs;
- must meet organizational goals as well as community goals;
- is a statement of your values;
- is a public declaration of outcomes;
- must be precise and practical;
- guide the actions of all involved;
- reflect the knowledge, philosophy and actions of the corporation;
- describes what you want to be in the future, contains compelling descriptions of how your organization will or should operate in the future, and explains how your clients will benefit from your service or product; and,
- must be positive and inspiring.

It does not define how the company will work but, rather, how it will look and act if the strategic plan is implemented correctly and successfully. It is a vision of future success -- communicates your strategic intent to employees and clients.

You will never be greater than the vision that guides you. Great leaders create great visions.

Values: governing the operation of your relationships with society, suppliers, employees, community, etc. The beliefs your organization members hold in common; commitment to excellence, innovation, creativity, honesty, etc.

Objectives: should be stated in terms of the results you want to achieve. Goals-specific time based measurements.

Strategies: a set of actions that enable an organization to achieve its objectives. They represent a way of comparing an organization's strengths with the changing environment.

Strategic Plan Content

1.   Introduction by President/Board Chair -- stamp of approval.
2.   Executive Summary -- reference mission and vision, highlights long term goals, states what is most important to the organization.
3.   Mission and Vision Statements.
4.   Organization profile and history -- key events, triumphs, changes.
5.   Critical issues -- a brief outline of ideas.
6.   Identify key strategies and major functioning areas.
7.   Program Goals and Objectives -- the vision and mission have answered the big question of why the organization exists, the goals and objectives are the plan of action (what you intend to do over the next year). Identify major achievable goals.
8.   Management goals and objectives.
9.   Strategies to achieve objectives.

Alice to the Queen: "I think I would have understood it better if I had written it down, but I can't quite follow it as you say it."

Strategic Plans:

- Relate to the medium term (2-4 years).
- Should be developed by owners /directors.
- Focus on matters of strategic importance.
- Are separated from day to day work.
- Should be realistic, detached and critical.
- Distinguish between cause and effect.
- Should be reviewed periodically.
- Are written down.

The plan is strategic because:

- It involves the setting of formal and mutually agreed upon goals.
- It lets you prepare for whatever circumstances arise.
- It leads to a thorough understanding of your business environment.
- It focuses attention on the business objectives, resources, problems and opportunities.
- It demands a certain order and discipline.
- It raises questions.
- It requires that you have a specific purpose in mind, and an understanding of your environment -- the forces that effect or

impede the fulfillment of your purpose and creativity in developing effective responses to the market forces.

- It forces management to think about **The Big Picture**.

Queen to Alice: "It's a poor sort of memory if it only works backward."

Successful strategic planning leads to:

- action
- inclusive ownership
- external focus
- shared vision
- acceptance of accountability
- quality data
- effective management

Implementation

1. Engage leadership -- involvement of senior personnel communicates a message of importance and priority.
2. Work from a common understanding -- list expectations and goals.
3. Include those who will be responsible to execute the plan.
4. Address critical issues for the organization.
5. Agree on how the plan will be actioned.

Competitive Analysis -- What the competition is doing that effects your business and your clients.

Situation Assessment -- External and internal stakeholders' perceptions about the company.

- An evaluation of impact on clients
- An evaluation of costs/benefits
- A data base of quality information
- Is the current vision being realized?
- Has the company's mission changed?
- Describe strategies used in the last few years and define outcomes
- How has the company been managed/funded?
- How have you sought to increase sales and share?

- How have productivity and costs moved?

1. Prepare and define the scope of your planning by reviewing previous plans.
2. SWOT.
3. Formulate strategies based on the above analysis.
4. Implement the strategies.
5. Communicate.

SWOT

1. What are the organization's internal strengths?
2. What are the organization's weaknesses?
3. What external opportunities might move you forward?
4. What external threats might hold you back?

Strengths and Weaknesses include:

- staff and board capabilities
- quality of programs
- products, reputation, management info
- financial systems
- office facilities/equipment

- sales
- marketing, distribution, promotion, support, management, expertise, systems, operations efficiency, capacity, processes
- products: quality, pricing, features, range, competitiveness, finances, resources
- performance, R&D, costs, systems

Threats and Opportunities

1. Industry where changes occur
2. Marketplace may be altering
3. Competition
4. New techniques and technology

Build on Strengths
Resolve Weaknesses
Exploit Opportunities
Avoid Threats

For want of a nail, the horse was lost;
for want of a horse, the battle was lost;
for want of a victory, a kingdom was lost;
And all for the want of a nail.

A company rarely fails or succeeds for trivial reasons. The causes are usually substantial, and are often self-evident to the outsider.

Queen to Alice: "Sometimes I've believed as many as six impossible things before breakfast."

Gathering the Intelligence

Alice: "Curiouser and curiouser...It would be nice if something made sense for a change."

Interview all board members and senior executives (questionnaires, telephone, in person). Include line staff!

Repeat with external stakeholders (clients, community leaders).

- Program outcome
- Inputs -- the resources required to operate
- Throughputs -- how the program is operated
- Outputs -- immediate, observable results
- Outcomes -- how the program affects clients' *lives*
- Impact -- benefit to client

How to Start

Doorknob to Alice: "Read the directions and directly you will be directed to the right direction."

- Obtain formal commitment – commitment of leadership.
- Select a planning committee of 5-7 people.
- Develop a work plan with specific responsibilities and time frames.
- Commit time and resources.
- Question the status quo.
- Assign resources and budgets.

Three Phases

Phase 1: Start Up

- Intelligence
- Segmentation
- Responsibilities

Phase 2: Diagnosis

- Internal and external systems
- Situation analysis
- Key issues

Phase 3: Strategy

- Mission and vision
- Strategies
- Action plan

The process ends with a new corporate mission, a new vision of the future, a review of management philosophy and implementation of the plan.

King to Alice: "Begin at the beginning and go on 'til you come to the end. Then stop."

Developing the Strategic Plan

THE MISSION STATEMENT

1. Define the purpose of your business.

   _____

   _____

   _____

   _____

2. What do you do?

   _____

   _____

   _____

   _____

3. What are your products/services?

   _____

   _____

   _____

   _____

4. What are you trying to accomplish?

_____

_____

_____

_____

5. What makes your business special?

_____

_____

_____

_____

6. What do you value as a corporation?

_____

_____

_____

_____

7. What is the ultimate result of your work?

_____

_____

_____

_____

BASED ON THE ABOVE, WRITE A 150-WORD
(MAXIMUM) STATEMENT OF YOUR BUSINESS.
MAKE EVERY WORD COUNT.

_____

_____

_____

_____

_____

_____

_____

_____

_____

_____

_____

_____

_____

_____

_____

THE VISION STATEMENT

8. What do you as a corporation believe in?

_____

_____

_____

_____

_____

9. What do you want the corporation to be in 3-5 years?

_____

_____

_____

_____

_____

10. What is your business philosophy?

_____

_____

_____

_____

_____

11. How will your clients benefit from the *future company*?

_____

_____

_____

_____

_____

BASED ON THE ABOVE, WRITE A BRIEF VISION STATEMENT. IT SHOULD BE POSITIVE AND INSPIRING!

_____

_____

_____

_____

_____

_____

_____

_____

_____

_____

12. What are the critical issues facing your company?

_____

_____

_____

_____

_____

_____

_____

_____

13. Define the objectives and goals of your company for the next year:

a) To _____

b) To _____

c) To _____

d) To _____

e) To _____

f) To _____

14. Develop strategies to accomplish each
    objective:

a) _____
b) _____
c) _____
d) _____
e) _____
f) _____

15. Competitive Analysis -- List all major
    competitors, assess their positions versus
    your company now and in the future; include
    strengths and weaknesses of each and how
    you will react to each.

(Attach.)

16. Implementing the plan:

a) Have you engaged all senior management in
    the process?

_____

b) Are you working from a common
    understanding?

_____

c)   Were those responsible for execution of the strategic plan involved in the development?

---

d)   Have you addressed all the critical issues facing the corporation?

WRITING YOUR BUSINESS PLAN

Easy 30 question format to a successful plan.

Writing the Business Plan

The hardest part of writing a business plan is getting started. At first, it seems like a daunting task, but just follow the steps listed below and it will come together...It always does!

First, you must decide why you are writing the plan. Is it to manage the business more effectively and efficiently? Or is it to raise capital?

Annual Plans are used to manage a business. Business Plans are usually written to raise money. Regardless, the plan becomes a written record of understanding your business at a point in time, understanding its structure, understanding its financial health, etc. It lets everyone involved in its execution know exactly what is expected of them. It is the nuts and bolts, how-to-get it-done-without-fail tool kit. It clearly sets out your corporate objectives for the year, and then describes how these objectives will be attained.

Interestingly, as you involve departments in the plans, the process develops bonds that may not have existed previously; it builds understanding and appreciation of other roles and departments. In fact, the real value of doing the plan is that it forces you to think about every facet of your business. Lastly, it is essential that everyone commit to the plan's implementation and success.

Throughout the writing, remember two things:

1. Write the plan as if everyone who reads it knows nothing about your company.

2. Write it with the intended audience in mind: investors, shareholders, customers. Remember that potential investors need a comprehensive and well thought out plan from which they will get a thorough understanding of your existing business, including the business itself, management, situation, market, fiscal reality, planning, rewards and risks.

And remember that a failure to plan, is a plan to fail!

Strategy

The first half of the plan will be geared to developing a solid business strategy -- the market, the industry, the customers, the benefits, the competition.

The second half of the plan is how to execute that strategy -- marketing, operations, products, services, etc.

Positioning...

...will define how you are going to present the company/product to the market place.

The plan will begin with an executive summary, but you will not write it until you have written the plan. We will outline at the conclusion of the profiler what should be included in the summary.

Remember not to over-reach with the plan -- it must be realistic and attainable. It has to work in the real world.

Ok. Let's get started!

Overview

1. Define your business/business concept.

_____

_____

_____

_____

2. Assess your company's current situation – successes, sales, problems, opportunities.

_____

_____

_____

_____

_____

_____

_____

_____

3. Outline your financial situation, financial health, total sales, profit, fiscal problems, opportunities, intended actions.

_____

_____

_____

_____

_____

_____

4. Briefly describe the history of your business. Include achievements and failures.

_____

_____

_____

_____

_____

_____

5. What are your business objectives?

_____

_____

_____

_____

_____

6. What is your business strategy? Why are you in business?

_____

_____

_____

_____

_____

_____

_____

7. Describe your product line, service offering. What makes your product unique? What are the product features? What key technologies are required for production?

_____

_____

_____

_____

_____

_____

8. Define the development stage of your business. Where do you want it to be a year from now?

_____

_____

_____

_____

_____

_____

_____

_____

_____

Operating Requirements

9. What are your facility requirements as to size, location, type of premises?

_____

_____

_____

_____

_____

_____

10. Provide a description of day-to-day operations.

_____

_____

_____

_____

_____

_____

_____

_____

Management

11. Give a detailed description of all senior managers – expertise, background, responsibilities.

_____

_____

_____

_____

_____

_____

12. Management positions to be filled.

_____

_____

_____

_____

_____

_____

_____

13. Current employment levels. Anticipated
     levels. Explain.

_____

_____

_____

_____

_____

_____

Mission

14. Clearly state your mission for the future of your company. What are you in business for?

_____

_____

_____

_____

_____

_____

_____

_____

> Note: Your mission statement is a cross between a slogan and an executive summary. It should be about 3 to 4 sentences in length. It should state who your company is, what you do, what you stand for and why. A clear and concise representation of the business's purpose for existence. Often, a mission statement is a one-liner, but is supported by a set of values. It can include concepts about your moral/ethical position, public image, target market, products/services, expectations, key strategic influence, or geographic domain. It is usually best developed after consultation with your senior staff. Avoid saying how great you are. And make sure that you actually believe in the final statement!

Market Analysis

15. What is your market share versus major competition? Is your share increasing, decreasing, the same as last year? Why?

_____

_____

_____

_____

_____

_____

16. List market segments/targets.

_____

_____

_____

_____

_____

_____

17. State size and maturity of the market and your position in it.

_____

_____

_____

_____

_____

_____

_____

18. List trends and seasonal effects.

_____

_____

_____

_____

_____

19. List the highlights of latest market research.

_____

_____

_____

_____

_____

20. Define customer characteristics/ demographics/needs. What do your customers value most?

_____

_____

_____

_____

_____

_____

_____

21. List industry problems, national/global events, legislation that affects business.

_____

_____

_____

_____

_____

_____

_____

SWOT

22. List your strengths, weaknesses, opportunities and threats.

Strengths

_____

_____

_____

Weaknesses

_____

_____

_____

Opportunities

_____

_____

_____

Threats

_____

_____

_____

Competitive Analysis

23. List your major competitors' strengths,
    weaknesses, and threats.

_____

_____

_____

_____

_____

_____

_____

_____

_____

Marketing

24. Describe how you intend to market your product. Planned advertising, promotion, website, brochures, etc. Include your projected budget.

_____

_____

_____

_____

_____

_____

_____

_____

_____

Sales

25. Describe your sales process – direct, warehouse, wholesalers, etc. How do the customers get your product? What sales training is required? Any industry trends?

_____

_____

_____

26. Detail total sales for the year and projections for the next 3-5 years.

_____

_____

_____

_____

_____

_____

27. Explain your pricing strategy.

_____

_____

_____

_____

_____

_____

Financial Disclosure

28. Include balance sheet, profit and loss statements, cash flow projections, summary of financial statements, operating budgets, income statements for the last 5 years, monthly projections, historical financial situation.

(Attach.)

Proforma income statements should show sales, cost of operations, profit (monthly and annually). Make sure that all financial numbers agree with other statements in the plan.

Note: If you are seeking start-up financing, has the market research been done? Has a prototype been made? Have facilities been leased? Is the management team in place? Are all plans finalized? If you are seeking expansion capital, you need to give clear evidence of a plan and not seek financing to solve problems or cover losses.

Legal and Regulatory Environment

29. Detail any licenses, copyrights, trademarks, patents.

_____

_____

_____

30. State any legislation, government regulations that affect industry.

_____

_____

_____

Don't forget to include any supporting documentation that is deemed pertinent, such as shareholder agreements, offers to purchase, letters of intent, memorandums of understanding, etc.

Executive Summary

Now you can write your executive summary and include it at the beginning of your Business Plan. It should not exceed one page. The summary should include:

- brief description of the business
- product or service uniqueness
- the market to be served
- competitive advantages
- your main objective
- important time frames
- key financial numbers

At the end, be sure and include business name and address, phone numbers, website, email, and principal names/contacts.

Sample Income Statement

	2014	2015	2016	2017	2018
Revenue					
Product/service					
Maintenance					
Consulting services					
Royalties					
Interest					
Other					
Total revenue					
Expenses					
Cost of goods sold					
Salaries re sales					
Other					
Gross margin					
Salaries					
Operating expenses					
Bad debt					
Contributions					
Depreciation					
Loan interest					
Other					
Total operating expenses					
Pre tax income					
Tax provision					
Net Profit					

BRAND PROFILE PLANNER

Definitions, The Laws of Branding, Why Brands Fail.

30 question format to help define and refine your brand.

Background

A brand is one of your most valuable corporate assets. In its simplest form, it is a word, symbol, term, design, colour or a combination of the above that instantly identifies your product or company, while creating an image in the hearts and minds of your target group.

Properly developed, maintained and nurtured, your brand is a clear, differentiating way to ask for consumer loyalty. It:

- is a promise of consistent quality and trust
- defines employee behavior
- positively affects price
- reduces communications costs
- builds awareness
- creates loyalty
- delivers a clear message
- confirms your credibility
- motivates action
- is the organizing principle of every action of the corporation

Products are made in a factory -- a brand is nurtured in the hearts and minds of the consumer. A product can be copied -- a brand is unique. A product can become outdated -- a brand is timeless. It is a cultural emblem in a shrinking world. It is a sustainable competitive advantage. It is sought out for purchase by your customer. It is a reason to buy.   It can and does become part of the user's life.

Your brand is pure **gold**, and should be treated as such at all times. It represents the entire experience your customer has with your company -- good and bad. It is easily damaged by a product problem, a careless employee remark, an unanswered phone, and a bad shopping experience. The brand lives or dies a little with each consumer contact.

Brands are distinct and recognizable, and there is never any confusion as to the space they occupy in the category. The brand should extend to every facet of your business and to every piece of communications. Its message must be consistent across all media. And your brand promise must be grounded in your core values and be able to create an emotional bond with your target group.

The above statements attest to the importance of a brand. They are a signal to the corporation to develop a strong brand and then never let it go.

After years of dealing with brands, I have developed the BRAND PROFILE PLANNER.

By answering the questions, you will be able to develop a truly meaningful brand, brand image, brand positioning, brand tonality, and brand character. Not to mention an unbeatable competitive advantage!

Definitions

Brand Image -- reflects the consumer perception of the brand. Your brand has an image whether you want one or not.

Brand Positioning Statement -- an inspirational statement of how you want the brand to be perceived. It defines your competitive advantage and gives the consumer a reason to purchase. It reflects the needs of the consumer. It speaks with a clear voice. It gives the brand a place to thrive.

A key positioning statement is to develop a point of advantage that resonates with the consumer and builds a relationship.

Ford: Quality is Job 1
American Express: Don't Leave Home Without It
Nike: Just Do It

Brand Character -- represents the moral and intellectual properties that distinguish the product from its competition. It usually has a direct link to the consumer, e.g., "Imperial Oil wears the white hat for the oil industry".

A brand that captures your mind, shapes behavior. A brand that captures your heart, gains commitment.

Brand Tonality -- the voice of the brand. Hallmark is a warm and caring company.

Brand Franchise -- the space it occupies in the consumer's consciousness. Volvo owns safety; Heinz owns tomato sauce; Xerox owns copying.

Brand Associations -- helps consumers process and retrieve information. They differentiate your product or service and create a positive attitude.

Brand Personality --

1. Sincere (Campbell's Soup); subsets: down-to-earth, family-oriented, honest, thoughtful, caring, wholesome, genuine, classic, sentimental, friendly.
2. Rugged (Marlboro); subsets: outdoorsy, masculine, western, active, athletic, tough, no nonsense.
3. Exciting (Benetton); subsets: daring, trendy, off-beat, provocative, young, lively.
4. Sophisticated (Mercedes); subsets: upper-class, charming, smooth, feminine.
5. Competent (IBM, Microsoft); subsets: reliable, intelligent, technical, serious, successful, a leader, confident.

Brand Identity -- how you aspire to be perceived. Consumers must know that you stand for something.

Brand Loyalty – cannot exist without purchase and use; but perceived quality, associations, and awareness can.

The silver bullets of the brand...Those words or phrases that should be part of every communication.

Why Brands Fail

Unless the brand is constantly nurtured, it will begin to fail. The reasons are usually:

a)   Consumers can't identify brand associations
b)   Lack of consistent use
c)   Lack of a brand champion
d)   Lack of long-term strategy
e)   Pressure to compete on price
f)   Brand proliferation
g)   Bias to change
h)   Lack of focus
i)   Character is allowed to erode
j)   Marketing efforts underfunded
k)   Brand extensions ill-conceived
l)   Brand loses touch with consumer needs
m)   Failure to properly service distributors
n)   Brand lacks cohesion across all mediums – advertising, packaging, point-of-sale, public relations

The Dozen Laws of Branding

1. The power of the brand is inversely proportional to its scope. A brand becomes stronger when it narrows its focus.
2. A brand should strive to own a word in the mind of the consumer.
3. A brand must have a claim to authenticity.
4. Quality is paramount.
5. A unique product needs a unique name.
6. The easiest way to destroy a brand is to put its name on everything.
7. What brands build, sub-brands destroy.
8. A brand is not built overnight.
9. A brand can be changed, but only carefully and very slowly.
10. The most important aspect of a brand is single-mindedness.
11. Brands live or die on contact with the consumer.
12. Remember -- Your customers do not show up for one mass meeting. Rather, they pass single file in front of your product in a constant parade of personal choice.

Brand Profile Planner

1. What is your company name?

_____

2. What is the brand name?

_____

3. How long has the brand been in existence?

_____

4. What does the company stand for?

_____

5. What does the brand stand for?

_____

_____

6. What are the brand attributes?

_____

_____

7. What are the brand associations?

_____

_____

8. Does the brand have an image? What is it?

_____

_____

_____

9. Does the brand have a positioning
statement? What is it?

_____

_____

_____

10. Does it have a voice? A tonality?

_____

_____

11. How does it differ from the competition?

_____

_____

_____

12. What are the specific customer benefits?

_____

_____

_____

13. Is the brand identity used across all segments of your business? What segments/divisions?

_____

14. Does the brand have a champion? Who is it?

_____

15. What is the current brand image? (It may not be the one you want.)

_____

_____

16. Who coordinates the brand's representations across all mediums?

_____

17. Does the brand have a consumer statement? What is it?

_____

_____

18. What is the brand personality? (sincere, exciting, rugged, etc.)

_____

_____

_____

_____

19. What is the brand's perceived quality?

_____

20. How would you rate customer loyalty?

_____

21. Does the brand position provide a rallying cry for your employees? Does it shape behavior?

_____

22. Would someone pay a premium for it?

_____

23. Does it hold a place in the consumers' consciousness? Heart?

_____

24. Where does your brand stand on this pyramid?

    Top of mind
    Brand recall
    Brand recognition
    Unknown

25. What are the product's functional benefits?

    _____

    _____

26. What are its emotional benefits?

    _____

    _____

27. What are your attentions versus intentions? (Attentions are what you are paying attention to; intentions are what you would like to pay attention to.)

Attentions

    _____

    _____

    _____

Intentions

_____

_____

_____

28. *Form follows function follows beliefs...*

What are your beliefs?

_____

What is the function of your product or service?

_____

_____

What form does it take?

_____

_____

29. What three words best describe your
    company's mission?

_____

_____

30. How important is your brand to your company's success? (Rate on a scale of 1 through 10.)

_____

_____

FOCUS
FOCUS

The number one reason businesses and senior executives fail.

Learn how to focus for success.

Failure to focus is one of the key reasons for business failure.

During my forty years in business and having worked with over 80 different companies -- many of which are leaders in their field -- I have witnessed companies, projects and people mired in the inability to start or complete tasks.

The problem is focus or, more correctly, lack of focus. And I believe it is one of the key reasons for business failure. If the work doesn't get out, the dollars don't come in.

The definition of focus is *the ability to concentrate on the right thing, to pay strict attention to the task, to concentrate long enough on one thing to get it done.*

My experience is that most people cannot do this. My initial belief was that you could not teach focus; however, after studying it for years, I now think it is possible to learn to be more focused. The failure to focus lies in bad business habits -- and those can be corrected. And along with a little self-discipline and the elimination of distractions, you can significantly improve your ability to focus on the task at hand. I urge you to master this ability!

The most common trait observed in accomplished people is an obsessive desire to completion. Once on a project they are compulsively driven to finish it. And they complete it quickly.

I once worked with a large software company owner on a non-work related project. He was terrific in the meetings, but the minute he left the meeting nothing of what he was supposed to do ever got done – not one thing in two years! He simply could not focus on the task. And I have seen dozens of examples of this behaviour. Why?

Most accomplishments boil down to one simple ability: focus. In fact, research has shown that focusing on more than one thing actually reduces productivity and jeopardizes the quality of work.

Better focus = better business!

Bad Business Practices

Here are the tell-tale signs of a lack of focus:

1.   Having trouble getting a proposal or presentation started. You simply can't find the time or motivation to sit down and start. It is so hard when contemplated and so easy when you do it. If you find yourself in this category, take immediate steps to correct it.

2.   Being consistently late with submissions... Everything is last minute, and these last minute self-induced panics are hard on your staff; and, they usually cost extra money. Get ahead of the task!

3.   Constantly on the phone -- made even worse by cell phones. Phones are the most insidious disrupter of focus. If you are a phoneaholic, STOP IT -- now! This is almost a disease. Get off you phone and onto your business. I can't emphasize this enough. If you are a phoneaholic, take steps to correct it.

4. Emailing the guy in the next office -- communicating with staff via email only is lazy and stupid...STOP IT -- now! Get off your ass and go and see your colleagues. Emails lack any form of creativity, and businesses thrive on interaction. I have seen this stifle many companies. Management by wandering around works -- so do it. The software company I mentioned above was guilty of this -- I forced the senior executives into the same room one day, and they were astounded at their own productivity and creativity.

5. Always too busy to get work done -- study after study has shown that people who are chronically busy are, in fact, not that busy. They are disorganized and unfocused. I have met a hundred of these types. If you are guilty of this, overcome the problem with scheduling, lists and organization. If your employees suffer from this, fire them!

6. Trouble prioritizing projects. Leads to missed opportunities.

7. Poor communications with staff and clients...breeds confusion.

8. Lack of clarity of direction from you...wastes staff time.

9. Taking work home on a consistent basis -- 8 hours a day is more than enough time to complete a project. (This relates to point 5.)

10. Taking your laptop on vacation. Don't. It's rude.

11. Poor listening skills are also a lack of focus. *"It's not that I am not interested in what you are saying, it's just that I can't hear you over the sound of my voice."* Teach yourself to listen.

12. Not remembering the names of people 20 seconds after you meet them is a lack of focus. Trick: repeat their name immediately.

13. Not doing what you promised is a lack of focus. Especially when other people are relying on you. Do what you say you are going to do.

14. Procrastination is the ultimate lack of focus! A word of advice: if you are procrastinating on something, 90% of the time it is something unpleasant and human nature

tries to avoid the pain. Do it first thing, get it out of the way, and chances are it will not be as bad as anticipated. And then you don't have to worry about it again.

IF ANY OR ALL OF THE ABOVE SOUND FAMILIAR, BEAR DOWN -- YOU ARE GOING TO HAVE TO LEARN TO FOCUS BEFORE IT IS TOO LATE!!!

Common blocks to focus are tired, bored, stressed, too many balls in the air, hunger, lack of clarity, avoidance.

You need to decide:

> What is my objective in doing the task?
> Clear the decks.
> Visualize the payoff.
> Be in the now.
> Write down what you're trying to avoid.
> Address it. NOW.

Be Consistent in Your Persistence

As mentioned, the hardest part of starting a task is, in fact, starting. So here is some very sound advice: Get started -- anywhere in the task...just get it rolling -- the inertia of keeping an object moving is far easier once that object is no longer stationary. You are that object. You don't have to start with page 1. But you do have to start.

When under pressure, an executive's weakest skill will fail first...and quite often, that is focus.

Charles Dickens wrote: *"I could not have done what I did without punctuality, order and diligence, and the determination to concentrate on one thing."*

Focus on what works, and stop doing what doesn't work. Spend time on relevant work!

A word on doing what you do best...

Let's say that you have the insight to say to yourself. "These are the three things I do really well in this task." So do them now and delegate the rest to those who have a different set of skills.

By doing your part, you have started the ball rolling.

Decide to Dump it, Delegate it, Defer it or Do it

Ask yourself what progress you can make today in completing a task, and do not take on a new project until it is completed. Know exactly what it is you wish to accomplish -- and be very specific. Divide the task into small pieces and focus on the bits.

F = Five More Rule

When you get bored or tired of the task before you quit, do 5 more...read 5 more pages, or answer 5 more questions, or study for 5 more minutes. You are stretching your attention span.

O = One Thing at a Time

Overcome perpetual preoccupation with what is on your mind -- make a deal with yourself, that you will deal with a particular item at precisely 4:30 p.m. and write it down so your brain doesn't have to. Then you are free to concentrate on the task at hand.

C = Conquer Procrastination

"It is amazing how long it takes to complete a task when you are not working on it." If you find yourself procrastinating on a task, ask yourself three questions:

1. Do I have to do this?
2. Do I want to do this so it is off my mind?
3. Will it be easier or harder to address later?

By answering the three questions, you will have made the determination. It really works!

U = Use your hands as blinkers to train yourself to tunnel vision

S = See the project clearly…as if for the first time

Pay attention to it. "Tell me what you are paying attention to, and I will tell you who you are." Clearly know what your attentions are versus your intentions; attention is what you are paying attention to, intention is what you are supposed to be paying attention to -- in this discussion, the task. "It is my intention to complete this proposal today."

Don't start with the problem, start with the solution. The full analysis of the problem is time-consuming and rarely, if ever, leads to the solution. Start by looking for a solution...as the chart below suggests, it is far more productive.

Problem Focus	Solution Focus
Past	Future
What is wrong	What is working
Blame	Progress
Control	Influence
Complication	Simplicity
Analysis	Action

Albert Einstein said: "You should make everything as simple as possible, but no simpler." (Even Einstein had to concentrate on the Theory of Relativity before he could move on to other tasks!)

"We are most productive when we concentrate on a very small number of things, on which we can devote a huge amount of time."
-- Albert Einstein

"My success, part of it certainly, is that I have focused on a few things."
-- Bill Gates

"What matters is where you want to go, focus is the right direction."
-- Donald Trump

"If you choose to hunt two wabbits, both will escape."
-- Elmer Fudd

"A successful warrior is an average man with laser-like focus."
-- Bruce Lee

Change only occurs when someone does something. Fire the first guy who says, "Someone should do something about this!"

It should come as no surprise that if you keep doing what you are doing, you will continue to get what you got.

You must avoid the infinite task loop: mosquito-type tasks that keep pulling you away from the big task. Set aside one hour a day for these distractions.

Use the moments -- I am not saying you have to focus on the task all day. You might have 20 minutes before a meeting, so focus for twenty minutes...no phone, no cell, no fax, no email, no visits -- no kidding! You can write a lot in 20 minutes!

Find another two hours in the early afternoon. Again, avoid all distractions...two hours is a huge amount of time when focused. HUGE. In fact, it is enough time to fully scope out the parameters of a task.

Once you start to learn to focus, your productivity will increase exponentially. In fact, once you learn to focus, the distractions will not distract you -- your laser beam mind will stay on target. And you should start in the early morning. By starting early, you can build momentum for the entire day. And, of course, the earlier you start a task, the less stress you will make for yourself.

As my Irish mother always said, "Never put off til' tomorrow what you can do today!"

A few thoughts before I close…

Management by wandering around works -- you learn everything and foster teamwork (versus emailing, which fosters absolutely nothing).

Leave your door open, encourage staff to come in. When they do, stop what you are doing immediately and focus on their request; do not keep your head down -- it is a sign of disrespect and suggests non-importance.

Never be late for a meeting -- this is another sign of disrespect and self- importance, not to mention disorganization. Focus!

Know staff names, who they are, and what they do. Focus! (A recognized employee is a loyal employee.)

Do not answer your cell phone during lunch. Or a meeting. It is a sign of disrespect. Focus on the task at hand and the person you are meeting with. (I have actually taken phones off people at lunch.)

Be prepared for everything. If you are focused, you will be ready!

Guess what? You can't do it all yourself. Hire good people.

By focusing the sun's rays through a magnifying glass, you can start a fire. That is how powerful focus can be...It can start fires.

Learn this simple ability, and you will succeed at everything you do.

Don Curtis has over 50 years experience in the marketing/advertising business in Canada, working with clients like McDonald's, Imperial Oil/Esso, London Life Freedom 55, in addition to over 70 other leading companies. See www.doncurtis.ca for details.